Eco Dogs

by Judith Bauer Stamper

Consultant: Samuel K. Wasser, Ph.D.
Center for Conservation Biology
University of Washington

New York, New York

Credits

Cover and Title Page, © Center for Conservation Biology/Sean Bogle; Cover TR, © Tim Chapman/KRT/Newscom; Cover CR, © Center for Conservation Biology; Cover BR, © Mark Sengelmann/National Park Service; TOC, © Working Dogs for Conservation; 4, © Janice Lynch/National Park Service; 5T, © Mark Sengelmann/National Park Service; 5B, © Melissa Farlow/Getty Images/National Geographic Images; 6, © Mark Sengelmann/National Park Service; 7, © Tim Chapman/KRT/Newscom; 8, © Pam Voth; 9, © David Parket/Omni-Photo Communications; 10L, © AP Images/J. Pat Carter; 10R, © Fred Minderman/National Park Service; 11, © Pam Voth; 12, © Brendan P. Kelly; 13T, © Brendan P. Kelly; 13B, © Brendan P. Kelly; 14L, © AP Images/Corpus Christie Caller-Times, Michael Zamora; 14R, © Padre Island National Seashore; 15, © Padre Island National Seashore; 16, Courtesy of Kathryn Purcell/USDA Forest Service/Pacific Southwest Research Station ; 17, Courtesy of Sam Wasser/Center for Conservation Biology; 18, © Courtesy of Sam Wasser/Center for Conservation Biology; 19, © Clay Myers/www.bestfriends.org/Courtesy of the Center for Conservation Biology; 20L, © Fred Felleman; 20R, © Maria Chantelle Tucker/Flickr/Getty Images; 21, © Fred Felleman; 22L, © Chris Bartos; 22R, © Poelking/Blickwinkel/Alamy; 23, © Chris Bartos; 24, © Alex Cornelissen/Sea Shepherd; 25L, © Andreas Eistert/WWF; 25R, © Andreas Eistert/WWF; 26, © Working Dogs for Conservation; 27, Courtesy of Conservation Canines at The Center for Conservation Biology; 28, © Center for Conservation Biology/Heath Smith; 29TL, © Eric Isselée/Shutterstock; 29TR, © Eric Isselée/Shutterstock; 29CL, © Eric Isselée/Shutterstock; 29CR, © Eric Isselée/Shutterstock; 29B, © Kelly Richardson Shutterstock.

Publisher: Kenn Goin
Senior Editor: Lisa Wiseman
Creative Director: Spencer Brinker
Design: Dawn Beard Creative
Photo Researcher: Amy Dunleavy

Library of Congress Cataloging-in-Publication Data

Stamper, Judith Bauer.
  Eco dogs / by Judith Bauer Stamper.
    p. cm. — (Dog heroes)
  Includes bibliographical references and index.
  ISBN-13: 978-1-61772-152-6 (library binding : alk. paper)
  ISBN-10: 1-61772-152-2 (library binding : alk. paper)
  1. Tracking dogs—Anecdotes. 2. Working dogs—Anecdotes. 3. Wildlife rescue—Anecdotes. 4. Endangered species. I. Title.
  SF428.75.S83 2011
  636.7'0886—dc22

                            2010041191

For more information, write to Bearport Publishing Company, Inc., 101 Fifth Avenue, Suite 6R, New York, New York 10003. Printed in the United States of America in North Mankato, Minnesota.

122010
10810CGF

10 9 8 7 6 5 4 3 2 1

Table of Contents

Python Pete

It was another hot, humid day in Florida, and Pete was on the hunt, **tracking** through the swamps of the **Everglades National Park**. Though Pete works in the park, he's not a park ranger. He's an **eco dog**.

Pete on the hunt with his owner and wildlife scientist, Lori Oberhofer

Pete spends his days with wildlife scientist Lori Oberhofer, searching for giant Burmese pythons. These snakes can grow up to be 20 feet (6 m) long. When Pete finds the scent of a python, he keeps his nose close to the ground, dragging Lori along on his leash. He also starts wagging his tail. Once they reach the snake, Pete pokes his nose into the grass. At that point, Lori pulls him away to keep him safe from becoming a snake snack. Lori then alerts rangers, who come to catch the python and remove it from the park.

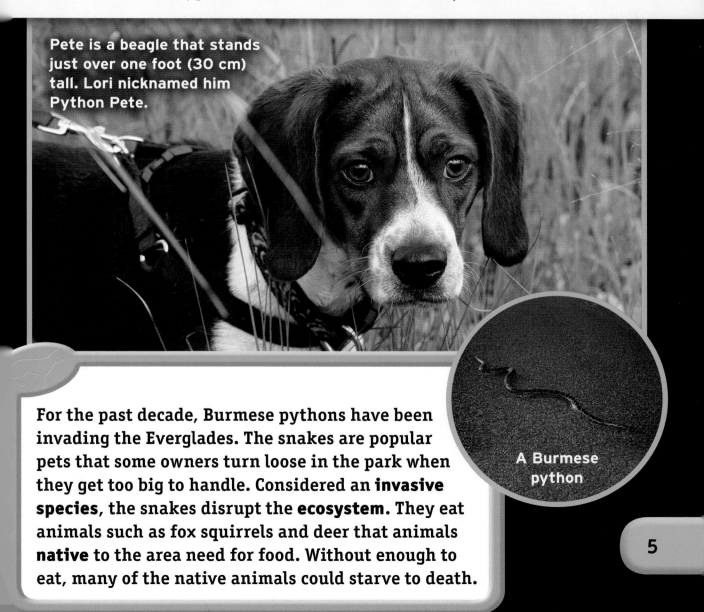

Pete is a beagle that stands just over one foot (30 cm) tall. Lori nicknamed him Python Pete.

A Burmese python

For the past decade, Burmese pythons have been invading the Everglades. The snakes are popular pets that some owners turn loose in the park when they get too big to handle. Considered an **invasive species**, the snakes disrupt the **ecosystem**. They eat animals such as fox squirrels and deer that animals **native** to the area need for food. Without enough to eat, many of the native animals could starve to death.

Hide-and-Seek

To get Pete ready for his job as an eco dog, he first had to learn what a python smelled like. To teach him the scent, Lori had Pete sniff a baby python and then gave him a treat. She did this over and over again. Not only did Pete learn the smell, but he started to connect the python with getting a reward.

Pete is not only Lori's partner, he's also her pet.

Pete's training took about three months to complete.

Once he knew the smell, Lori put a live python in a bag and dragged it across a field to create a **scent trail**. Then she hid the bagged python at the end of the trail, along with Pete's favorite toy—a small stuffed animal. Pete quickly learned to follow the trail to find the bag and toy. The toy was his reward for finding the python.

Pete began training with Lori when he was just a puppy.

7

Super Sniffers

Python Pete and other eco dogs are part of a new group of **detection dogs**. These heroic hounds use their super sense of smell to sniff out plants and animals that scientists aren't able to find on their own. Many of these plants and animals are **endangered**. Because of the dogs' hard work, scientists are now able to learn more about these plants and animals and find ways to save them. Or in Pete's case, save animals that are at risk of becoming endangered.

How can Pete and other eco dogs find certain kinds of plants and animals that humans cannot? Dogs have about 225 million **scent receptors** in their noses, compared to humans who only have about 5 million. These receptors, plus other parts of a dog's nose and brain, help it smell 10,000 to 100,000 times better than a person. How good is Pete's sense of smell? He can tell the difference between the scent of a Burmese python and the scent of other types of snakes that live in the Everglades.

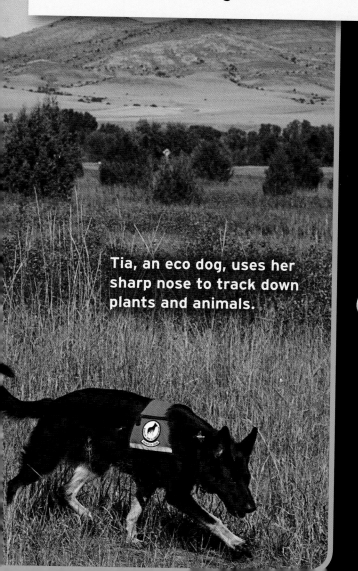

Tia, an eco dog, uses her sharp nose to track down plants and animals.

"Eco dog" is short for ecology dog. Ecology is the study of the relationship between plants, animals, and their environment.

Training

Not every pup can be trained to become an eco dog. Trainers look for animals that are good searchers and are very focused on getting a reward for finding things. Basic training can take from four weeks to up to a few months. Though eco dogs are trained in many different ways, training usually starts with a dog learning the smell of the animal or plant it will be tracking. The pup does this by sniffing the actual animal or plant—or something with its scent—over and over again.

Pete sniffs a young python in order to learn its scent.

Pete, with Lori, following a scent trail during training

Dogs such as Pete are tracking dogs. They are trained to track down a scent trail by keeping their noses down. They do this because they're searching for the scent of an animal that's been left behind on the ground.

Other dogs, called air scent dogs, follow the scents of animals and plants that are carried in the air. To do so, they are trained to keep their noses high in the air, moving in the direction where the scent is strongest. Whether a tracking dog or an air scent dog, both types are always rewarded with a favorite toy when the animal or plant is found.

Trainers use a special toy, such as a rubber ball, to reward an eco dog for a job well done. The same toy is usually used both during training and on the job.

Some eco dogs come from animal shelters. They are too high-energy to be household pets, but they love to be outdoors tracking down scents.

Labs on Ice

After an eco dog finishes basic training, it will usually join a team of scientists on a **conservation** mission in the United States or elsewhere in the world. These missions often land the dogs in surprising places. For example, Jamberry, a black Labrador retriever (Lab), is on an eco-mission in the **Arctic**.

Jamberry

Jamberry works closely with Dr. Brendan Kelly, a research scientist who studies how the decreasing sea ice in the Arctic affects ringed seals. Dr. Kelly has trained Jamberry to find the seals' breathing holes by following the seals' scent. When he finds the scent, Jamberry runs toward it in a zig-zag pattern. Once at the breathing hole, he starts digging. Dr. Kelly then calls the dog back and sets up a net over the hole to capture the seal when it comes up for air. Once the seal is captured, scientists attach a **satellite tag** to it and return the animal to the water. This lets them track the seal so they can learn more about its movements.

Dr. Kelly at a breathing hole with Jamberry (left) and Reba (right)

Jamberry and other Labs working with Dr. Kelly find 100 to 200 breathing holes a month.

Jamberry and Dr. Kelly searching for breathing holes

Beach Patrol

Ridley, a Cairn terrier, is another hard-working eco dog. He works alongside Dr. Donna Shaver on the beaches of Padre Island National Seashore in Texas. The beaches are a breeding ground for the rare Kemp's Ridley sea turtle, a species that is near **extinction**. Ridley started out as Dr. Shaver's pet. Now he's her partner.

Newly born Kemp's Ridley sea turtles

Ridley and Dr. Shaver

Ridley helps Dr. Shaver locate nests where each female sea turtle has buried 100 or so eggs in the sand before swimming back into the sea. At first, when he smells a nest, Ridley alerts Dr. Shaver by digging gently in the sand, so he doesn't hurt the eggs. Then he sits back and waits for his treat. Dr. Shaver gathers the eggs and takes them to a laboratory to hatch, where they will be safe from **predators** and bad weather. Later, when they are old enough, she takes the baby sea turtles back to the beach, where they slowly walk into the water and swim safely away.

Ridley finds a sea turtle nest hidden in the sand.

Kemp's Ridley turtles are the most endangered of all sea turtles. Their population began decreasing in 1947. However, since scientists such as Dr. Shaver have begun protecting their eggs, the sea turtles' population is on the rise.

Scat Trackers

Some **threatened** and endangered animals such as bears and tigers are hard for scientists to find. They move quickly across large areas and hide out in thick forests or **remote** mountains. However, every animal leaves behind a trail of **scat**, which eco dogs can easily locate. Scientists have discovered that they can learn a lot about an animal by studying the **DNA** and **hormones** found in its body waste.

Mocha, an eco dog, locates the scat of fishers, medium-size animals that belong to the weasel family. After she finds some scat, her handler smells it to make sure it's fresh. Scientists can't use old scat because it no longer contains the DNA and hormones they need for their research.

One of the first scientists to study DNA and hormones in animal scat was biologist Dr. Sam Wasser. By **analyzing** the scat samples, Dr. Wasser was able to learn about an animal's health, including its diet. Scientists can also use information from scat to determine if an animal species is in danger because of changes in its habitat—such as the loss of food sources or disease outbreaks.

Moja, shown here, was the first eco dog Dr. Wasser trained to find scat.

Eco dogs that locate scat are usually larger breeds such as Labrador retrievers and German shepherds. These dogs have long legs that are strong and allow them to quickly search four to five miles (6.4 to 8 km) a day over rocky land, looking for scat.

17

The Scat Team

Dr. Sam Wasser now heads up the Center for Conservation Biology at the University of Washington. The center's mission is to study how changes in the environment, such as cutting down large forests, affect wildlife. The center is home to scientists and a scat team made up of about 15 detection dogs.

At the Center, the eco dogs live in a state-of-the-art doghouse with 16 indoor and outdoor **runs**. The house sits on 4,300 acres (1,740 hectares) of land, which is plenty of space for training dogs for real-life missions. The dogs also have a play area and training classrooms.

The dogs' housing is in the middle of Pack Forest, where trainers take the dogs out for scat hunts.

It takes the dogs about one month to be fully trained. Each one learns the scent of up to 12 different species. For example, Alli, an Australian cattle dog mix, has been trained to find the scent of wolverines, wolves, grizzly bears, American martens, Sierra red foxes, and Pacific pocket mice.

Here, Alli has found a scat sample.

The Center gets its dogs from animal rescue centers and shelters. They look for dogs that have lots of energy and like to search and retrieve things.

A Whale of a Tail

Most scat-tracking dogs work on land, but Tucker's job takes him out to sea. Most days, this black Lab can be found on the front of a research boat, wearing a bright yellow life jacket. Tucker is an expert at sniffing the scat of orcas, or killer whales, that live in Puget Sound in Washington State. The number of orcas living in the waters there has been dropping—and scientists are worried. They study orca scat to see if it contains chemicals from pollution or if it shows that the whales aren't finding enough to eat.

An orca

Tucker, shown here at sea, was trained at the Center for Conservation Biology.

Once Tucker catches the scent of orca scat, he leans over the front of the boat. His ears change position, his mouth opens, and his tail starts wagging excitedly. For Tucker, finding scat means getting to play with his ball, his reward for a job well done. After scientists collect the scat, Tucker goes right back to work.

Tucker wears a life jacket in case he accidentally falls into the water. Here, he is on alert as he spots whale scat.

Tucker is the best Lab that the orca scientists have worked with. He always keeps his mind on the job and doesn't want to swim in the ocean! Unlike most Labs, he's afraid of the water.

Cheetah Dog

On the other side of the world from Tucker, a Border collie named Finn is helping save cheetahs in the African country of Namibia. The cheetah is the fastest land animal on the planet, but it's also the most endangered cat in Africa.

A cheetah can run at a top speed of about 70 miles per hour (113 kph).

Finn in Namibia

Finn works with scientists from the Cheetah Conservation Fund (CCF), a group whose mission is to conserve and protect cheetahs. Finn and the scientists go out into the cheetahs' natural habitat to search for scat. When Finn finds a sample, the scientists take a **GPS** reading of the location and collect the scat. Then they analyze the scat to learn what the cheetahs' **range** is and how the animals reproduce. Most important, the scientists use DNA analysis of the scat to keep track of how many cheetahs there are in the wild and to find out if their population is increasing or decreasing.

Finn searching for cheetah scat

Finn isn't the only dog helping to protect the cheetahs' population in Namibia. Scientists at CCF give farmers guard dogs that keep cheetahs away from livestock by barking loudly. As a result, farmers are less likely to lose livestock and kill cheetahs.

Smugglers Beware!

Most eco dogs work in nature. There are some, however, that work in airports, on docks, and at borders. These dogs have a very important job—to stop people from smuggling endangered animals or their body parts into other countries.

An eco dog checks luggage at an airport.

Amy, a German shepherd, and Uno, a Lab, work at the Frankfurt International Airport in Germany. Animal smugglers from Southeast Asia, Africa, and Latin America often go through this airport. The two dogs are trained to sniff luggage and bags for the scent of feathers, reptiles, ivory, and bone. So far, the dogs have stopped smugglers from taking rhino horns, elephant tusks, shark fins, and a live iguana out of the country.

Amy

Wildlife smuggling also poses a serious danger to animals from the tropical forests of Central and South America. Airport detection dogs have caught smugglers with rare parrots, monkeys, snakes, and lizards.

By using dogs such as Uno, shown here, and Amy, airport officials want to show smugglers that they will be caught if they try to transport endangered animals out of the country and into other ones. Officials hope this will stop the smugglers from harming the animals in the first place.

A Scientist's Best Friend

Eco dogs have been at work for only a short time, but already they've become very important detection dogs. They are accurate, quick to learn, and make great members of scientific teams. Due to the dogs' hard work, animals from grizzly bears to killer whales to African elephants are safer.

Wicket, an eco dog, set a record for finding the most scat in one day— 47 bear scat samples!

The future looks bright for eco dogs. Many scientists think that detecting chemicals in wildlife or in scat will be one of the most important jobs for eco dogs. For example, the detection of a new chemical in animal scat might mean pollution is increasing. Or finding a rare plant with special chemicals might lead to a cure for a human disease. Every year, scientists are discovering more and more ways that these dogs can help save Earth and its animals!

Scooby, shown here with scientist Jennifer White, has been trained to find jaguar scat as well as scat from many other animals.

Most eco dogs work until they are eight or nine years old.

Just the Facts

- Detection dogs can be trained to find almost anything that has a scent. Eco dogs can search for things such as eggs, mushrooms, weeds, chemicals, birds, and elephant tusks.

- Eco dogs save scientists time and money. How? They search faster than humans do, go into places that machines can't reach, and require little maintenance.

- Not all eco dogs come from shelters. Some are already working dogs, having gotten their start as drug or bomb detection dogs.

- Eco dogs that are trained at the Center for Conservation Biology train for seven days a week. Once out in the field, they work for eight to ten hours a day. They get every third day off to rest.

Border collie

beagle

Cairn terrier

German shepherd

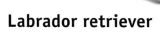

Labrador retriever

analyzing (AN-uh-lize-ing) examining something carefully in order to understand it

Arctic (ARK-tic) the northernmost area on Earth; one of the coldest areas in the world

conservation (*kon*-sur-VAY-shuhn) the protection of wildlife and natural resources

detection dogs (di-TEKT-shuhn DAWGZ) types of dogs used to find things such as bombs and drugs

DNA (DEE-EN-AY) short for deoxyribonucleic acid; the molecule that carries the genetic code for a living thing

eco dog (EE-koh DAWG) a dog that works with scientists, helping them find certain animals and plants

ecosystem (EE-koh-*siss*-tuhm) a community of animals and plants that depend on one another to live

endangered (en-DAYN-jurd) being in danger of dying out

Everglades National Park (EV-ur-*glaydz* NASH-uh-nuhl PARK) a wetland area in southern Florida

extinction (eg-STINGKT-shuhn) when a type of animal has died out

GPS (GEE-PEE-ESS) a space-based navigation satellite system that provides accurate location information

hormones (HOR-mohnz) chemicals that are made by certain glands in a person or animal's body

invasive species (in-VAY-siv SPEE-sheez) plants and animals that have been brought to an area where they aren't normally found

native (NAY-tiv) naturally born and living in a particular place

predators (PRED-uh-turz) animals that hunt and kill other animals for food

range (RAYNJ) the distance over which an animal travels

remote (ri-MOHT) far away; hard to get to

runs (RUHNZ) enclosures for animals to move around in

satellite tag (SAT-uh-*lite* TAG) a device that sends signals to a spacecraft orbiting Earth, which then sends the signals back to Earth; used to track the movements of an animal

scat (SKAT) body waste from an animal

scent receptors (SENT ri-SEP-turz) special cells in the nose that are used for smelling

scent trail (SENT TRAYL) a scented path that animals follow in order to locate things such as food

threatened (THRET-uhnd) being in immediate danger

tracking (TRAK-ing) following the path or trail of someone or something

Bibliography

Halfpenny, James. *Scats and Tracks of North America: A Field Guide to the Signs of Nearly 150 Wildlife Species.* Guildford, CT: FalconGuides (2008).

Helton, William S., ed. *Canine Ergonomics: The Science of Working Dogs.* Boca Raton, FL: CRC Press (2009).

Horowitz, Alexandra. *Inside of a Dog: What Dogs See, Smell, and Know.* New York: Simon & Schuster (2009).

Read More

Collard, Sneed B. *Science Warriors: The Battle Against Invasive Species.* Boston, MA: Houghton Mifflin Books (2008).

Dendy, Leslie. *Tracks, Scats, and Signs.* Milwaukee, WI: Gareth Stevens Publishing (2000).

Learn More Online

Visit these Web sites to learn more about eco dogs:

conservationbiology.net/conservation-canines/faq/

www.cheetah.org

www.nps.gov/kidszone/nps_dogs.html

About the Author

Judith Bauer Stamper writes fiction and nonfiction books for children. Many of her books are about animals. She lives in New Jersey but grew up on a farm in Ohio, where she had working dogs as pets.